Chicago Lincoln Statue, Lincoln Square

The John and Mary Jane Hoellen
Chicago History Collection
Chicago Public Library

AUG – – 2004

CHICAGO

UNIVERSE

Published in the United States of America in
2003 by UNIVERSE PUBLISHING

A Division of Rizzoli International Publications, Inc.

300 Park Avenue South, New York, NY 10010

Revised edition of *Chicago*, first published in the
United States of America in 1987 by Rizzoli
International Publications, Inc.

2003 2004 2005 2006 / 10 9 8 7 6 5 4 3 2 1

Library of Congress Control Number:
2003104734

Design by Opto Design

Printed in China

(Cover) Chicago skyline at sunset from
North Beach.

(Pages 2–3) Chicagoans enjoying a game
at Wrigley Field.

(Pages 6–7) Gold Coast high-rise apartments
above Oak Street Beach.

DEDICATION
To Gayla, Ivon, and Tony

ACKNOWLEDGMENTS

Going back to Chicago was a great experience,
especially seeing many old friends and meeting
new ones who pointed me in the right direction
and smoothed the path before me. Kudos to
Mayor Richard M. Daley, who is helping to make
Chicago the Paris of America.

I want to thank my Santa Barbara friends, Susan
and Paul Singer, and Susan Ellefson of the
Fairmont Hotel for making my stay comfortable.

Other people who gave special help include Mark
Spencer of Sears Tower, Larry Hill of Chicago
University, Marsha and Bob Rosner, Catherine
Dolce, Donna La Pietra, Cheryl A. Bachand of the
Frederick C. Robie House, Amanda Enser of the
Shedd Aquarium, Renee Jessup of the Museum
of Contemporary Art, Nancy O'Shea of the Field
Museum, Kathleen Schreiber of the Chicago
Mercantile Exchange, and an army of security
guards who led me to countless windy roofs.
Appreciation goes also to Paolo Namias of *Zoom*
magazine for his thoughtful suggestions.

A very special thank you goes to Michael Jungert
for the hours of invaluable time and effort he
spent during the shooting of this book.
Appreciation goes to Bill Kurtis for sharing with
me his love for Chicago, and above all, for honor-
ing me with the foreword to this book. I also
want to thank my publisher, Charles Miers, my
editors Alex Tart and Holly Rothman, and Opto
Design for a job well done.

CHIC

PHOTOGRAPHS BY SANTI VISALLI | FOREWORD BY BILL KURTIS

CAGO

Chicago is a great American city. Perhaps it is the last of the great American cities.

NORMAN MAILER,
*MIAMI AND THE SIEGE
OF CHICAGO*, 1968

There's a new Chicago rising. It's bursting through old buildings in the Loop to create sparkling glass canyons. It's sprouting towers of poured concrete in empty railroad yards and crawling into skeletons of aging factories to replace the blue collars with white. Even the early sun seems to dance lightly over the sharp new angles in its skyline. And its sound—the sound that hums from the neighborhoods and ball parks and scaffolds is the sound of renewal.

It's not the first time Chicago has changed. Every great city is always growing and dying at the same time: "Building, breaking, rebuilding," as Carl Sandburg described Chicago in 1916. He was the child of immigrant parents who came out of the prairie to behold this giant by the lake with a sense of wonder. Skyscrapers that others would take for granted and disparage, he exalted. Where they would see another overgrown industrial city, Sandburg saw "a tall bold slugger set vivid against the little soft cities."

Sometimes it takes a visitor to show us the change. Someone who can see it with fresh eyes. Someone like Santi Visalli. His photographs depict a city we knew was there but had not seen so clearly before. Armed with his cameras, this photojournalist arrived, as others have, anxious to record the monuments of Louis Sullivan, Frank Lloyd Wright, and Ludwig Mies van der Rohe. But he was transfixed by the works of a "new" generation of the Chicago School of Architecture.

In the short span of a few decades, the city has added a special meaning to its own invention—the skyscraper—with a building that reaches higher than any other in the world and, in its shadow, a translucent cavern where government workers cluster on open ledges like ancient cave dwellers seeking shelter from winter storms. The combination of glass and steel is so striking in its vision of the future that we are thankful for Visalli's photographs—almost afraid that, like Brigadoon, the structures will vanish suddenly, only to rise again in another hundred years from an obscure onion patch in the tall grass prairie of America's middle belt.

The fear may not be totally unfounded. Ironically, the new Chicago has taken almost exactly that long to materialize.

It started with a fire. Whether it really began in Mrs. O'Leary's barn doesn't seem to matter now, but we do know she was milking her cow by the light of a kerosene lantern. Her barn was crowded among frame buildings constructed almost entirely of wood. The cow could easily have kicked the lamp into the dry straw to provide the ignition for a firestorm that swept over 15,768 buildings and killed 300 men, women, and children. The fire began October 8, 1871, and when it finally burned itself out, Chicago's claim to being a city was reduced to ghostly images of broken masonry walls standing above smoking ashes.

Chicagoans measure time from the Great Fire. In countless ways, they still live with decisions made in the days that followed the city's greatest crisis. Within a month, the city elected an extremely able mayor, Joseph Medill, publisher of the *Chicago Tribune*. In his inaugural address, he set the course for strong architectural development by discouraging paper and tar roofs, urging instead "materials as incombustible as brick, stone, iron, or slate."

The city's cultural commitment might be traced to the outpouring of sympathy from thousands of readers around the world who sent books to restock the city's library. Their gifts were placed in an empty water tank above the temporary City Hall. Because it was a favorite pigeon roost, its name, "The Rookery," would survive each new building erected on the site.

Three days after the fire, the directors of the Chicago Board of Trade resolved to build "the most costly and ornamental structure of its kind in the world" at Jackson and La Salle streets, anchoring a financial box canyon within the Loop and establishing a thriving trading community that would be growing long after Chicago ceased to be the Hog Butcher for the World. And even before the embers of the Great Fire were cool, Marshall Field reopened for business in the stables of the streetcar company.

So it began. As if a lightning stroke had cleansed the ancient prairie, new shapes quickly sprouted from Chicago's ashes. Brick cottages replaced the wooden-frame shacks. Ornate marble was shaped to the front of granite and sandstone mansions along European boulevards. The city seemed to be rushing to catch up with the rest of the nation, afraid it would miss the expansion into the West. But when it paused long enough to catch its breath, Chicago found itself in the middle of everything, at the head of navigation of the Great Lakes, at the center of the nation's richest coal fields, in the heart of the Mississippi Valley farmlands, at the hub of the nation's railroads. "Even on a trip to the pearly gates," they would say, "you have to change trains in Chicago."

At the end of twenty years, this sweating, stormy frontier settlement had become all of Sandburg's metaphors: "Hog Butcher for the World, Tool Maker, Stacker of Wheat, Player with Railroads and the Nation's Freight Handler." Chicago had pulled off one of the greatest recoveries of all time and now wanted to brag about it.

On the occasion of the four-hundredth anniversary of the landing of Columbus in America, this rural upstart invited Paris, London, Rome, Tokyo, Berlin, Vienna, Peking—the centers of art, science, royalty, and wealth of the world—to help celebrate. Despite this breathtaking audacity, the World's Columbian Exposition of 1893 evolved into an unparalleled convocation. It came at the height of what artists, scientists, architects, and industrialists believed was an American Renaissance. And it took only one look at the enormous exhibition halls of the "White City," patterned on the world's great architecture, to confirm the sense that America was the legitimate heir to Italy's sixteenth-century accomplishments. When Daniel Burnham, chief of construction of the Exposition, later unveiled his Plan of Chicago, the future seemed clear: Chicago would be one of the world's great cities.

Almost a hundred years later, Burnham's Plan is world famous. His fingerprints can be found on the parks, streets, and grand boulevards of Chicago, providing a framework inside which the city has evolved. Santi Visalli's photographs measure that evolution from the windowless shell of the once prosperous residency hotel of Al Capone, which has since been demolished, to award-winning skyscrapers in another section of town. Whole neighborhoods have disappeared as others explode with new forms. And some never seem to change, as if protected by an unseen guardian.

When Visalli found such architectural giants of Chicago's past as the Adler and Sullivan Auditorium Building still competing for attention with the gaudy newcomers to the Loop, it was as if Daniel Burnham were there, his presence lingering over the city like a Lake Michigan fog on a cold morning. And when Visalli captured a lake inferno on the verge of consuming the Adler Planetarium, it was like seeing Burnham's passion made visible as his city rose in the dawn.

This city by the lake can have that effect on you. And it can change its moods with the light. Theodore Dreiser preferred the Chicago evening, "that mystic period

WORKERS' COTTAGES ON CORTLAND STEET.

between the glare and gloom of the world when life is changing from one sphere or condition to another." Nelson Algren remembered the "nights when the blood-red neon of the tavern legends tether the arc-lamps to all the puddles left from last night's rain, somewhere between the bright carnival of the boulevards and the dark girders of the El."

Algren lived on Chicago's Wild Side, which has changed least of any part of the city. Whiskey has lost its bootleg attraction but is still king of the night, challenged only by cocaine as the sinner's quickest poison. Guitars and harmonicas that once poured their sounds out the doors of gin mills and apartments to pay the rent today are amplified and heard around the world. They are changing the pulse of the city from the staccato of Capone's machine gun to the pounding beat of Chicago Blues. But violence still staggers mindlessly down the alleys. In the slums, you can still find the marks of wanton hunger on the faces of women and children, and like Sandburg, you can see the gunman kill and go free to kill again.

And yet, for every shudder of the Big Shoulders, there is a soft surprise—like the delicate watercolor pastels Visalli found when the May sun splashed its morning light across Oak Street Beach. And there is what Visalli calls the "tangible culture" that grows beneath the austere towers of steel and cement: the works of Picasso, Miró, Calder, Chagall, and Henry Moore, not sheltered behind Gothic columns for a few but hugging the sidewalks for the people in the finest public art gallery in the country.

It was inevitable that the faces of Chicago would change, too, as the neighborhoods shifted their character. Irish, Germans, Italians, and Poles stirred rich cultures into Chicago's melting pot. While you can still eat pierogis on Milwaukee Avenue without hearing English

spoken, many of the Europeans who came to Packingtown for work, who laid the sewers and built the city, have seen their children move to suburbs. New immigrants have come to blend Hispanic and Asian faces with Chicago's black population. Now, the ethnic tapestry is even more colorful and more representative of the nations of the world.

A Cambodian woman proudly showed me a tiny urban garden she had scratched out of a vacant lot in Uptown. Her family had escaped the terrors of war by walking hundreds of miles to the safety of Thailand where they waited in refugee camps to be sent to America—and Chicago. She reached down to the growing plants and picked several tiny seeds. Then, in broken English, she explained how she had carried a few such seeds in her dress all the way from the other side of the world so she could plant them in her new home. No plants like these had ever grown in Chicago before, but they were thriving, even in the soil of a vacant lot still mixed with broken glass and splinters. Everything about her was different, except her story. Chicago has heard it millions of times in different ways as it goes on building, breaking, rebuilding, always making room for someone else to tell the story.

The Chicago revealed in these photographs will look different from any previously documented, but even her most futuristic structures are inescapably linked to a past when her citizens dreamed of building a city from ashes and had the temerity to plan "the greatest city in the world." The new Chicago documented by Santi Visalli is proof their dreams are still alive and growing.

MICHIGAN AVENUE, THE
"MAGNIFICENT MILE"

Gigantic, willful, young, Chicago sitteth at the northwest gates.

WILLIAM VAUGHN MOODY,
"AN ODE IN TIME
OF HESITATION," 1901

(ABOVE) VIEW NORTH FROM THE LOOP TOWARD NORTH MICHIGAN AVENUE AND LAKE MICHIGAN.
(PAGES 14–15) MAX ADLER PLANETARIUM (1930), EAST END OF ACHSAH BOND,
ERNEST A. GRUNSFELD, ARCHITECT, ON A COLD NOVEMBER DAY.

(ABOVE) LAKE POINT TOWER (1968), EAST GRAND AVENUE.

(ABOVE) ALARM CLOCKS (*REVIEILS*) BY FERNANDEZ ARMAN AT THE MUSEUM OF CONTEMPORARY ART.

(TOP) C. D. PEACOCK JEWELRY STORE, PALMER HOUSE (1927).
(BOTTOM) CHICAGO BOARD OF TRADE (1930), 141 WEST JACKSON BOULEVARD, HOLABIRD AND ROOT, ARCHITECTS.

(TOP) 35 EAST WACKER DRIVE (1926).
(BOTTOM) CLOCK AT BANK ONE PLAZA LOOP.

(ABOVE) SKYLINE WITH GRANT PARK.

(PAGE 26) CHICAGO RIVER BETWEEN 35 EAST WACKER DRIVE (1926),
CENTER, AND MARINA CITY (1964, 1967), RIGHT.
(PAGE 27) SKYLINE WITH JOHN HANCOCK CENTER.

25

(ABOVE) HOMAGE TO THE CHICAGO SCHOOL OF ARCHITECTURE (1980) BY RICHARD HAAS, 1211 NORTH LA SALLE STREET; FROM LEFT, FRANK LLOYD WRIGHT, JOHN W. ROOT, DANIEL BURNHAM, AND LOUIS H. SULLIVAN.

BURNHAM

SULLIVAN

(PAGE 30) RISING ABOVE THE MORNING FOG ARE, FROM LEFT, THE FIRST
NATIONAL BANK OF CHICAGO (1969), PERKINS & WILL, ARCHITECTS; THE IBM BUILDING
(1971), LUDWIG MIES VAN DER ROHE, ARCHITECT; MARINA CITY; AND SEARS TOWER.
(PAGE 31) SEARS TOWER ON A FOGGY DAY.

(ABOVE) *THE FOUR SEASONS* (1974), BY MARC CHAGALL, ON FIRST NATIONAL PLAZA.

33

I adore Chicago. It is the pulse of America.

SARAH BERNHARDT

(RIGHT) LYRIC OPERA OF CHICAGO ON OPENING NIGHT.
(PAGES 36–37) CARSON PIRIE SCOTT & CO., STATE AND MADISON STREETS, ORNAMENT BY LOUIS H. SULLIVAN.

(ABOVE) DETAIL OF THE ROOKERY BUILDING (1886), 209 SOUTH LA SALLE STREET, BURNHAM AND ROOT, ARCHITECTS.

(PAGE 40) KRAUSE MUSIC STORE FACADE (1922), 1611 NORTH LINCOLN
AVENUE, WILLIAM C. PRESTO WITH LOUIS H. SULLIVAN, ARCHITECTS.
(PAGE 41) WRIGLEY BUILDING (1919–21), NORTH MICHIGAN AVENUE, DETAIL.

(ABOVE) THE SPECTACULAR LIGHT DISPLAY AT BUCKINGHAM FOUNTAIN CAN BE ENJOYED EVERY EVENING IN GRANT PARK DURING THE SPRING, SUMMER, AND FALL MONTHS.

(PAGE 44) A GILDED STATUE OF THOMAS JEFFERSON AT THE EDGE OF THE LOOP. (PAGE 45) COLONNADE OF UNION STATION (1917), CANAL STREET BETWEEN ADAMS STREET AND JACKSON BOULEVARD, DESIGNED BY GRAHAM, BURNHAM AND COMPANY.

(PAGES 46–48) CROWDS GATHER DAILY AT PIZZERIA UNO, WHERE CHICAGO'S FABULOUS PIZZA ORIGINATED.
(ABOVE) SIGNS OF CONTEMPORARY BUSINESSES ADORN THE HOTEL ST. BENEDICT FLATS (1882–83). THIS PRIME
EXAMPLE OF VICTORIAN GOTHIC, DESIGNED BY JAMES J. EGAN, WAS THE FIRST APARTMENT BUILDING
IN CHICAGO BUILT IN THE CHIC BROWNSTONE STYLE.

(ABOVE) SOUTH FACADE OF THE ART INSTITUTE OF CHICAGO (1892), MICHIGAN AVENUE,
SHEPLEY, RUTAN AND COOLIDGE, ARCHITECTS.

(ABOVE) SKYLINE FROM NORTH BEACH.

(PAGE 54) THIS VIEW OF THE MIRACLE MILE (MICHIGAN AVENUE) FEATURES A STATUE
OF FAMOUS SPORTSCASTER SAM BRICKHOUSE IN THE FOREGROUND.
(PAGE 55) SKYLINE FROM SEARS TOWER.

My first day in Chicago, September 4, 1983. I set foot in this city, and just walking down the street, it was like roots, like the motherland. I knew I belonged here.

OPRAH WINFREY

(RIGHT) INTERIOR OF *MONUMENT WITH STANDING BEAST* (1984), BY JEAN DUBUFFET, STATE OF ILLINOIS CENTER.

(ABOVE) INTERIOR OF THE CHICAGO THEATER.

(PAGE 60) THIS SPIRAL STAIRCASE WITH A KOI POND AT ITS BASE IS AN OUTSTANDING FEATURE OF THE MUSEUM OF CONTEMPORARY ART. DESIGNED BY JOSEF PAUL KLEIHUES, THE MUSEUM IS ONE OF THE NATION'S LARGEST FACILITIES DEVOTED TO THE ART OF OUR TIME. (PAGE 61) MCCORMICK MANSION (1893), MCKIM, MEAD AND WHITE, ARCHITECTS.

(PAGES 62–63) CHANDELIER DECORATED WITH FISH MOTIFS AT THE SHEDD AQUARIUM.

(ABOVE) A POPULAR FEATURE AT THE SHEDD AQUARIUM IS THE DOLPHIN SHOW, HELD
IN A GLASS-ENCLOSED ROOM DESIGNED BY LOHAN ASSOCIATES AS AN ADDITION TO
THE ORIGINAL BUILDING, DESIGNED BY GRAHAM ANDERSON.

(LEFT) POLAR BEAR AT LINCOLN PARK ZOO.
(ABOVE) THE MAGICAL LINCOLN PARK CONSERVATORY DISPLAYS BOTANICAL BEAUTY YEAR-ROUND.
(PAGES 68–69) SUE, THE MOST POPULAR GIRL IN CHICAGO, IS FORTY-TWO FEET LONG AND TWELVE FEET TALL. SOME SIXTY-FIVE MILLION YEARS AGO SHE WEIGHED ABOUT SEVEN TONS BUT NOW IS DOWN TO THREE THOUSAND POUNDS.

(PAGES 70–71) MUSEUM CAMPUS.

(ABOVE) THE MAGNIFICENT FIFTEEN-STORY FERRIS WHEEL IS AN OUTSTANDING FEATURE OF THE NAVY PIER. THIS FIFTY-ACRE COMPLEX ON THE LAKEFRONT JUST NORTH OF THE CHICAGO RIVER ALSO HAS PROMENADES, GARDENS, SHOPS, RESTAURANTS, AN OUTDOOR PERFORMANCE PAVILION, A SHAKESPEARE THEATER, THE CHICAGO CHILDREN'S MUSEUM, AND MANY OTHER FORMS OF FAMILY ENTERTAINMENT.

(ABOVE TOP, BOTTOM, AND PAGE 77 TOP) ORNATE FANLIGHTS IN THE GOLD COAST.

(ABOVE BOTTOM) FANLIGHT OF 60 CEDAR STREET.
(PAGE 78) MERCHANDISE MART (1930) VIEWED FROM LA SALLE STREET BRIDGE.
(PAGE 79) OLD DRAWBRIDGE FRAMING SKYLINE OVER CHICAGO RIVER, ALONG WACKER DRIVE.

Perhaps the most typically American place in America.

JAMES BRYCE, 1888

(RIGHT) OLD WATER TOWER, NORTH MICHIGAN AVENUE AT CHICAGO AVENUE.
(PAGES 82–83) FAIRMONT HOTEL LOBBY.

(ABOVE) JOHN HANCOCK CENTER (1969), NORTH MICHIGAN AVENUE BETWEEN
CHESTNUT AND DELAWARE STREETS, SKIDMORE, OWINGS & MERRILL, ARCHITECTS.

(ABOVE) THE MAX PALEVSKY RESIDENTIAL COMMONS (2001), DESIGNED BY RICARDO LEGORRETA, STANDS IN STARK CONTRAST TO THE TRADITIONAL GOTHIC BUILDINGS AT THE UNIVERSITY OF CHICAGO.

(PAGE 88) GARDEN OF THE ART INSTITUTE OF CHICAGO.
(PAGE 89) BUCKINGHAM FOUNTAIN, GRANT PARK.

87

(ABOVE) SCONCE IN LOBBY OF PALMER HOUSE.
(RIGHT) WILLIAM W. KIMBALL HOUSE (1890–92) SOUTH PRAIRIE AVENUE BETWEEN 18TH AND 20TH STREETS.

(ABOVE AND RIGHT) THE FREDERICK C. ROBIE HOUSE (1909), 5757 SOUTH WOODLAND AVENUE, A MASTERPIECE OF FRANK LLOYD WRIGHT'S PRAIRIE STYLE, IS BEING RESTORED BY THE FLW PRESERVATION TRUST. ITS BOLD HORIZONTAL LINES, DARING CANTILEVERS, STRETCHES OF ART-GLASS WINDOWS, AND OPEN-FLOOR PLAN INSPIRED AN ARCHITECTURAL REVOLUTION.

(ABOVE) FLOOR OF STATE OF ILLINOIS CENTER.

(ABOVE) SKYWARD VIEW OF 150 NORTH MICHIGAN AVENUE.
(RIGHT) FACADE OF CHICAGO METROPOLITAN CORRECTIONAL CENTER (1975), VAN BUREN STREET BETWEEN CLARK
AND FEDERAL STREETS, HARRY WEESE AND ASSOCIATES, ARCHITECTS.

(LEFT) CHICAGO THEATER (1921), 175 NORTH STATE STREET, C. W. AND GEORGE L. RAPP, ARCHITECTS.
(ABOVE) THE JOHN BANDY QUARTET PLAYS AT ANDY'S JAZZ CLUB, ONE OF MANY THAT DRAW CHICAGO JAZZ LOVERS.

(ABOVE) ORNATE TILE DECORATION ON A CHINATOWN RESTAURANT.

(ABOVE) PAGODA OF ON LEONG CHINESE MERCHANTS' ASSOCIATION (1930),
2216 SOUTH WENTWORTH AVENUE, MICHAELSEN AND ROGNSTAD, ARCHITECTS.

101

(ABOVE) MURAL IN PILSEN.
(RIGHT) A PRE-COLUMBIAN–STYLE MURAL IN PILSEN.

Chicago will give you a chance. The sporting spirit is the spirit of Chicago.

LINCOLN STEFFENS
*THE AUTOBIOGRAPHY
OF LINCOLN
STEFFENS, 1931*

(RIGHT) FRENETIC ACTIVITY IS THE ORDER OF THE DAY AT THE CHICAGO MERCANTILE EXCHANGE, WHERE FUTURES AND OPTIONS HAVE BEEN TRADED SINCE 1898.

(PAGES 106–107) MARINA CITY (1964, 1967), THE RIVER BETWEEN STATE AND DEARBORN STREETS,
BERTRAND GOLDBERG ASSOCIATES, DETAIL OF FACADE.
(ABOVE) GARAGE AT THE MARINA BUILDING.

(ABOVE) UNIVERSITY OF CHICAGO CAMPUS.
(LEFT) GENERAL GRANT AND PADDLEBOAT RIDER, LINCOLN PARK.
(PAGE 112) TOWN HOUSE, ASTOR STREET.
(PAGE 113) IVY-COVERED TOWN HOUSE.

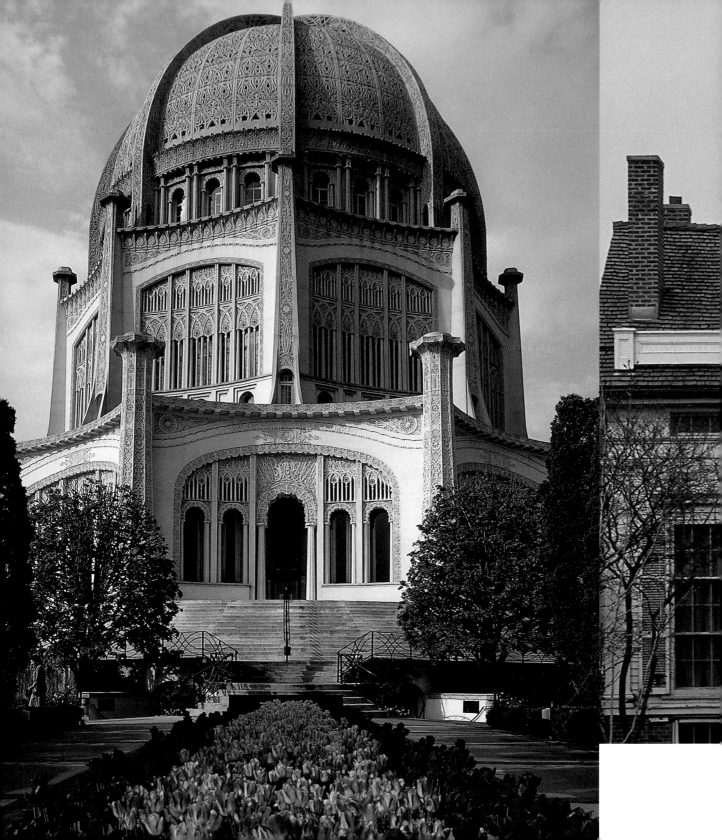

(LEFT) BAHA'I HOUSE OF WORSHIP (1920–53), WILMETTE, ILLINOIS.
(ABOVE) THE WIDOW CLARK HOUSE, AT 410 WEST HURON STREET, IS THE OLDEST EXTANT BUILDING IN CHICAGO.

(ABOVE) FACADE AND CORNICE OF RAILWAY EXCHANGE BUILDING, SOUTH MICHIGAN AVENUE.
(RIGHT) WRIGLEY BUILDING.

(PAGES 118–119) SKYLINE.

(ABOVE) MOON OVER CHICAGO, VIEWED FROM THE MAX ADLER PLANETARIUM.

(ABOVE) NIGHT VIEW OF SPAGHETTI JUNCTION, INTERCHANGE OF DWIGHT D. EISENHOWER, JOHN F. KENNEDY, AND DAN RYAN EXPRESSWAYS.

(LEFT) A "WINDOW IN THE SKY" IS PART OF THE AMA BUILDING DESIGNED BY I. M. PEI AT STATE AND ILLINOIS. (ABOVE) DETAIL OF FACADE, PEOPLE'S GAS, LIGHT AND COKE CO.

(ABOVE) VIEWING THE SKYLINE FROM THE PLANETARIUM IS A FAVORITE ACTIVITY OF CHICAGOANS AND TOURISTS ALIKE.

(PAGE 128) SKYLINE FROM THE PLANETARIUM, WITH THE ASSOCIATED BUILDING, PRUDENTIAL BUILDING,
ONE PRUDENTIAL PLAZA, AND THE AON BUILDING

127